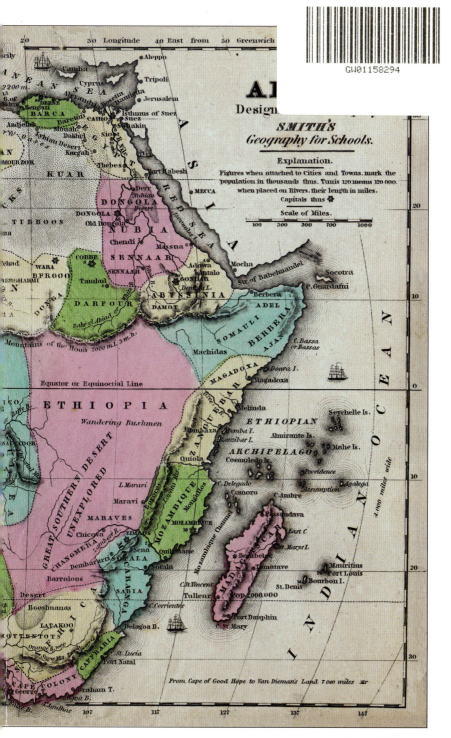

Africa - 1839

ENFIELD
and the Transatlantic Slave Trade
1807 — 2007

Edited by Valerie W. Munday.
Researched by Nigel Sadler, Valerie Munday,
Dr Kathleen Chater and Jan Metcalfe.

This booklet is produced as part of a major exhibition to mark the 200th Anniversary of the Parliamentary Abolition of the Transatlantic Slave Trade and its links to Enfield.

www.enfield.gov.uk

Copyright © Enfield Museum Service 2008

All rights reserved. No part of this book may be reproduced in any form without written permission from the publisher.

Unless otherwise credited all images are supplied by Sands of Time Consultancy. www.sandsoftimeconsultancy.com

Booklet design by Nigel Kellaway

ISBN 0-906076-02-1

A catalogue record of this book is available from the British Library.

Published by

Enfield Museum Service
PO Box 58
EN1 3XJ

www.enfield.gov.uk/museum

EMS, Enfield Museum Service, numbers in brackets, refer to objects held in the Museum Service's collection.

Front Cover: West India Docks, London. Taken from an engraving by Augustus Pugin and Thomas Rowlandson (image courtesy of Ian Jones).

Back cover: Bush Hill Park (EMS Ba1560). Watercolour dated 1834. Bush Hill Park (later called the Clock House).

Contents

10 - Acknowledgements
11 - Foreword

Part I - History of Slavery

12 - Africa
16 - The African Slave Trade
20 - The Enslavement of Africans
24 - Slave Ships
28 - The Triangular Trade
30 - Liberated Africans
34 - Slavery in the Caribbean
38 - Slavery in South America
42 - Slavery in the USA
46 - Slavery in Britain
50 - British Anti-Slavery Movement

Part II - Enfield at the time of the Transatlantic Slave Trade

54 - Quakers and Abolition
58 - Famous Quakers at Winchmore Hill
62 - Parish Churches
66 - The Parish of Enfield
70 - The Parish of Edmonton
74 - Black People in Enfield
78 - Connections with the Slave Trade
84 - A Georgian Study
88 - Sylvia Woodcock

Part III - Slavery Now and its Legacy

92 - Slavery 1834 to Today
96 - Legacy of Slavery

100 - Further Reading and Sources
102 - Index
107 - Dates of the Abolition of Slavery

*This book is dedicated to my
mother Winifred Munday (1922-2007).*

Acknowledgements

Enfield and the Transatlantic Slave Trade

This booklet has its origins in an exhibition which was developed from a discussion between Nigel Sadler and Valerie Munday on how the bicentenary of the Parlimentary Abolition of the Transatlantic Slave Trade could be commemorated in the London Borough of Enfield.

The exhibition would not have been possible without the support of Enfield Racial Equality Council (EREC) who facilitated a steering group for the exhibition:

Ken Allen, Enfield Caribbean Association
Margaret Amor, The Friends Meeting House, Winchmore Hill
Kate Anolue, Councillor LBE
Sam Bell, EREC
Chandra Batia, CEO of EREC
Bevin Betton, Chair of EREC
Peter Brown, Enfield Library Service
Martha Osamor, African Women's Welfare Association
Marcia Sinclair, School Improvement, Education, Learning & Community Services
Roger Hallam, EREC
Valerie Munday, Enfield Museum Service
Nisha Patel, EREC representative
Nigel Sadler, Sands of Time Consultancy

I should like to thank Enfield Museum Service who prepared and developed the exhibition and gave assistance with the booklet without whom it would not have been possible:

John Griffin, Documentation Assistant;
Emily Jost, Museum Education Officer;
Jan Metcalfe, Community Museum Officer

Also I should like to thank:

Nigel Sadler, Sands of Time Consultancy; Dr Kathleen Chater; Ruby Galili;
Graham Dalling and Kate Godfrey, Local History Unit, LBE
Simon O'Connor, Photographer; Nigel Kellaway, Designer
Ian Jones, Sam Bell and Monica Smith for loan of their objects for use in the booklet.
Julie Gibson, Head of the Library and Museum Service;
Sue Kirby, for her help in proof reading the text.

Julie Hudson, Claude Ardouin, Fiona Grisdale and Frances Carey who facilitated the loan of objects from the British Museum
Joanna Clark, The Library of the Religious Society of Friends
Gill Warnell, Nancy Brobbey and Rosalind Munday-Thompson and colleagues and volunteers at Forty Hall Museum for help with the exhibition.
The Heritage Lottery Fund for generously supporting the exhibition and booklet.

Valerie Munday, Museum Development Manager, Enfield Museum Service

Foreword

2007 commemorated the 200th anniversary of the Parliamentary Abolition of the Transatlantic Slave Trade. The Act of 1807 outlawed the Transatlantic Slave Trade and made it illegal for British ships to be involved in the trade.

However it would be almost another 30 years, in 1834, before slavery itself was finally abolished throughout the British Empire and not until 1838 that the apprenticeship system (slavery in all but name) was abandoned.

The bicentenary offered the opportunity to remember the millions who lost their lives as well as those who suffered. It also allowed us to pay tribute to the courage and moral conviction of all those ordinary people, both black and white, as well as politicians, who resisted and campaigned to end slavery.

The 1807 Act marked an important point in this country's development towards the nation it is today.

The commemoration is an opportunity to reflect on the fact that there are still throughout the world today an estimated 20 million people suffering the daily reality of modern slavery.

Although this exploitation is often not called slavery, the conditions are the same. People are sold like objects, forced to work for little or no pay and are at the mercy of their 'employers'.

Slavery exists today despite the fact that it is banned in most of the countries where it is practised. It is also prohibited by the 1948 and the 1956 UN Supplementary Convention on the Abolition of Slavery, the Slave Trade and Institutions and Practices Similar to Slavery.

Women from Asia and Eastern Europe, some of whom will end up in Enfield, are bonded into prostitution, children are trafficked between West African countries and men are forced to work as slaves on Brazilian agricultural estates.

Contemporary slavery takes various forms and affects people of all ages, sex and race.

So whilst we rightly commemorate the 200th anniversary of the abolition of the transatlantic slave trade, we must also use the occasion to recognise the slavery that continues to exist today and be inspired by the example of those who acted in 1807.

Councillor Paul McCannah

Cabinet Member for Leisure, Culture and Olympics

February 2008

Africa

Traditional wooden carving of a crocodile from Gambia. The carving is standing on a wax printed fabric. This type of fabric is widely used in West Africa for clothing for men, women and children. The designs on the material often have significant meanings. This fabric shows the symbol Gye Nyame meaning 'Except God - God is supreme'.

images: Simon O'Connor

Traditional Wooden Headdress. Worn by the women of the Mende Tribe of Sierra Leone. Mid 20th Century. Object courtesy of Sam Bell.

A Civilised Continent

Africa is home to one of the first great civilisations, the Ancient Egyptians (c3000-332BC). Less well-known are the succession of empires (Ghana, Mali and Songhay) in West Africa between the 8th-16th centuries. These states were largely dependent on the gold-salt trade across the Sahara and the establishment of trade routes across West Africa. By the 11th century Muslim traders controlled these routes and widespread conversion to Islam followed. Timbuktu emerged as a key trading post and was a centre of Islamic learning attracting scholars to the new mosques, universities and libraries.

During the period of the Transatlantic Slave Trade there were several major kingdoms in West Africa including the Akan (Asante) in Ghana, the Yoruba Oyo kingdom in Nigeria and the Kingdom of Dahomey, present day Republic of Benin.

Akan

From the 15th-late 17th century, the Akans people in Ghana controlled gold mining and trade in West Africa. The rise of the Asante in the 18th century shifted the focus of this trade to the royal court at Kumase. Akan (Twi-speaking) brass casters produced huge numbers of brass weights and paraphernalia for measuring and storing gold.

The most significant cultural object among the Asante remains the Golden Stool. Another important cultural symbol is Kente cloth.

Gold guinea and quarter guinea coins of George III and George I. Coins like these took the name 'guinea' from the Guinea Coast in West Africa where the gold was mined. (EMS Ba140-7)

Yoruba

Yorubaland has consisted of several independent kingdoms. Among these, the ancient city of Ife is at the centre of religious and political power for the Yoruba people. The terracotta and metal sculptural masterpieces dating from 12-15th centuries at Ife coincided with the commercial expansion of the neighbouring city-state of Oyo. Ife is associated with Yoruba religious traditions that have influenced the African Diaspora cultures in the Americas. Prominent Yoruba deities include 'Ibeji' (protector of twins), 'Osun' (Goddess of fertility, protector of children and mothers) and 'Sango' (God of Thunder).

The Kingdom of Benin

Oral traditions link the origin of the Kingdom of Benin in the 13th century with its neighbour, Ife, probably through the introduction of metal-casting techniques. For 500 years Benin generated exquisite art. By the late 1400s a wealthy royal court supported a city of metal smiths, carvers and other craftsman.

The Kingdom of Danhomè (Dahomey)

In the Bight of Benin, the Fon kingdom of Danhomè took control of two rival states, Allada and Xwéda (Ouidah), in the early 18th century, forming the powerful Kingdom of Danhomè (modern Republic of Benin). Danhomè was a strictly militaristic culture resulting in frequent wars with its neighbours. Its military strength was ensured by exchanging weapons with European traders for captured slaves. Today people in the Republic of Benin share certain cultural links with communities in Haiti, Cuba and Brazil (the Vodun religion) while descendants of slaves repatriated to Benin have introduced religious practices to Africa such as worship of the Brazilian 'Mamiwata' (water goddess).

Asante Brass gold-weight. Mid 20th century. Reproduction weight from Ghana used for weighing gold. The weight shows two people playing Mancala or Ayo, a count and capture game. It is played in various forms throughout Africa and in many other regions of the world. Goldweights were used by the Akan peoples of Ghana for weighing gold dust and nuggets. Most goldweights were cast using the 'lost wax' (cire perdue) method. They were then adjusted to the correct weight by adding molten lead into cavities. Object courtesy of Monica Smith.

A half size copy of an Asante stool (EMS 2007.14.1) from Ghana, on a piece of Kente cloth, (EMS 2007.14.4). The Golden Stool is believed to incorporate the spirit of the Asante nation and symbolise its unity. The symbol in the centre of the stool reads Gye Nyame which means 'Except God'.

The African Slave Trade

A slave shed, Congo.

History of Slavery

Slavery is known from the earliest periods. The oldest surviving written laws, Hammurabi's Law Code (c1780 BC) produced in Babylon, Ancient Mesopotamia (modern Iraq) distinguishes between free men, serfs and slaves. Religious texts have also distinguished between free people and slaves. The Babylonians, Egyptians, Greeks, Romans and the Ottomans all used slaves to develop their empires.

The Pyramids at Giza. The Egyptian dynasties sometimes utilised enslaved labour in their grand construction schemes. According to the Bible, Moses lead the Jews from slavery in Egypt to the Promised Land.

Slavery in Africa

African societies all utilised slaves. These were often individuals who were criminals or troublemakers or captured warriors sold into slavery. In many cases the only other option to enslaving these people was execution or ritual sacrifice.

The First European Exploitation

Once Europeans discovered West Africa's potential for trade, the fate of the Africans was sealed. Greed and ruthless efficiency saw the Europeans fighting for control, making alliances with African kings and building their own forts for protection.

The Portuguese were the first European power to exploit Africans and then to transport them across the Atlantic. Other European countries became involved to meet the demand for labour in their newly discovered territories in the Americas. John Hawkins (1532-1595), a cousin of Sir Francis Drake, is recorded as the first British slave trader. Between 1562 and 1567 he made four journeys from the Sierra Leone River to Hispaniola (modern day Haiti/Dominican Republic) taking 1200 Africans to sell to the Spanish settlers.

It was not just Africans who were enslaved. Pierre Joseph Dumont was a French man enslaved in Africa from 1781-1816. White Europeans were captured by Muslims off the coast of North Africa. They could work for their freedom through payment or conversion to Islam.

West Africa

The end of the European slave trade did not see the end of European influence in enslaved labour. In 1885 King Leopold II of Belgium established the Congo Free State. He controlled a period of murder, torture and enslavement to raise greater profit from rubber production. Millions of Congolese are said to have been killed or worked to death during Leopold's control of the territory. The campaign, led by British diplomat Roger Casement (1864- 1916), revealed the truth and became the first mass human rights movement.

East Africa

Slavery was not only present in West Africa, it was widespread throughout the African continent. After the European powers outlawed slavery there was still a flourishing slave trade in East Africa which the British tried to end with varying degrees of success.

Today, throughout the African continent there are areas where slavery still exists. In 2003 Mende Nazer published her experience of being a slave in Sudan.

Zanzibar slave market, c1909

The Enslavement of Africans

A sanitised drawing of a slave post where enslaved Africans were gathered together for sale.

Capture of Slaves

Prior to contact with Europeans, slavery as a source of forced labour played a role in some of the local economies. Enslavement was often the result of a punishment for crime, or as payment for a debt; capture and enslavement also occurred through warfare. In most cases the status of the slaves was framed by local customs. Slaves were also used as retainers to safeguard vulnerable boundaries or to help conquer new territories. However, the arrival of European traders led to the transformation of these practices through the development of a lucrative trade in captives in exchange for firearms, metal, imported cloths, tobacco, etc. At the height of this trade in the 17th-18th centuries, the increased demand for slaves was fulfilled through increased military activity, raids and by kidnapping.

Many Africans died or were murdered on the walk, whilst the women often suffered physical and sexual abuse.

The captured Africans had to walk to the coast, in some cases many hundreds of miles.

Slave March

Before they reached the coast the captured victims were forced to endure long marches, shackled together. They were often bought and sold several times along the way.

Slave Warehouse/Trunk

After their long forced march the captured Africans were placed into a slave warehouse, or trunk. Initially these were owned by the kings of the local tribes but later they were managed by slave traders. Conditions in these warehouses were horrific.

Slave Forts

Captives were held at coastal forts, often for several months, before boarding ships to take them to the New World. Numerous forts were built by the competing European powers along the Atlantic coast from the late 15th century onwards. In the Gold Coast (modern Ghana) alone, 30 forts were constructed to hold slaves.

Slave Fort, Cape Coast Castle, Ghana as it stands today.

Elmina Castle in modern Ghana was the largest of these forts and became a notorious centre for the slave trade. It was built by the Portuguese in 1482 and seized by the Dutch in 1637, before it eventually passed to British control in the late 19th century. Enslaved Africans were held in the castle, before being led through the infamous 'Door of No Return' to board the slave ships.

Loading of the Enslaved Africans

During the purchase process and loading, the enslaved Africans were carefully monitored by the ship's doctor, to ensure they did not have any diseases. The Africans would be taken from the slave fort or slave warehouse to waiting canoes. The canoes then carried them to the ship. Many tried to jump to freedom before being taken down to the ship's hold. Those who tried to escape often drowned.

Captured Africans being carried in a canoe

Slave Ships

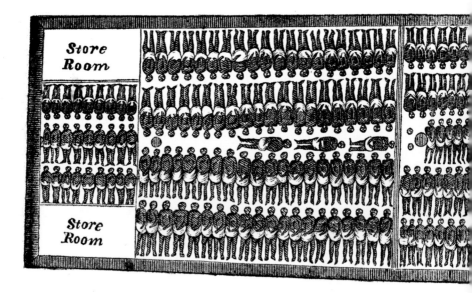

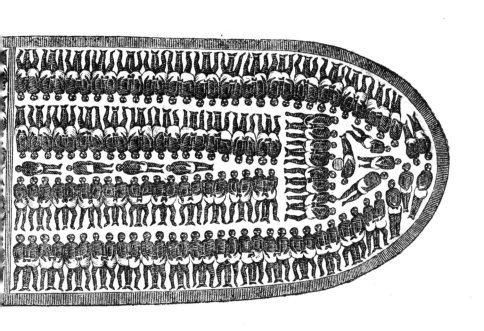

Thomas Clarkson commissioned a drawing of the slave ship *Brookes* to show the barbaric conditions the Africans suffered.

Tightly Packed

Conditions on the slave ships were horrific. The enslaved Africans were onboard ship for two to three months, during the Atlantic crossing. They were often tightly packed and chained together with all bodily functions taking place where they were chained. This level of sanitation meant disease was rife and the smell of human suffering was overpowering; an approaching slave ship could be smelt from 5 miles away. In the hold the enslaved Africans died where they lay, and their bodies remained chained to fellow Africans, sometimes for several days. A quarter of the estimated 12 million Africans shipped across the Atlantic, died during the crossing. As dead or dying slaves were thrown overboard, most slave ship records state that sharks were constant companions during the journey.

Branding of an enslaved African before boarding a slave ship.

Most deaths were through disease or punishment but some Africans were deliberately murdered. In 1781 the captain of the slave ship Zong threw 133 Africans overboard because drinking water was running out and he thought the insurance company would cover the loss. If the Africans had arrived dead the owners would receive no insurance money. In Britain two court cases debated this insurance claim, the argument centring on the loss of property not loss of life! The Anti-Slavery Campaigner Granville Sharp wanted the crew tried for murder but he was not successful. The insurance claim also failed. This incident was famously depicted by the painter J.M.W. Turner (1775-1851) in 'Slave ship - slavers overthrowing the dead and the dying - typhoon coming on'.

Reproduction slave tag. The inscription reads 'MALE BLACK AFRICAN HEATHEN No. 102'. The reverse side reads 'BRIGG ROYAL CHARLOTTE 1770'.

On board some ships the women were continually sexually abused by the male crew members whilst on others the captains maintained order and made sure the Africans had regular exercise and food. Some did this for moral reasons, others for financial reasons - the better the enslaved Africans were treated the greater chance the owners had of making a bigger profit.

Enslaved Africans on board ship, wearing slave tags for indentification.

On Board Revolts

It is not surprising that revolts occured on one in ten slave ships. To keep control, the crew treated any disobedience harshly. This included whipping the Africans, cutting off limbs and even throwing them into the sea to drown. As an act of resistance, some enslaved Africans committed suicide or killed their young infants by throwing them into the sea.

Local Trading Vessels

There were also ships that included enslaved people as a small part of a general cargo. Mary Prince, an enslaved African (c. 1788-?), recorded her journey from Bermuda to the Caribbean in 1802. 'We were nearly four weeks on the voyage, which was unusually long. Sometimes we had a light breeze, sometimes a great calm, and the ship made no way; so that our provisions and water ran very low, and we were put upon short allowance. I should almost have been starved had it not been for the kindness of a Blackman called Anthony, and his wife, who had brought their own victuals, and shared them with me.'

The Triangular Trade

The 'Triangular Trade' is the term used to describe the three-legged trade. The first leg saw slave ships loaded with European products sailing from Britain to Africa. The second saw trade items from Africa, mostly enslaved people, taken to the Americas. This second leg of the journey has been known as the Middle Passage as it sees the process from a European viewpoint. For the enslaved Africans it was their first passage so today the term Transatlantic Passage is preferred. The final leg saw the slave ships loaded with Caribbean products returning to Britain.

 On Route to Africa   **On Route to the Americas**

Guns/Gunpowder

Alcohol

Enslaved Africans

Cowrie Shells

Glass Beads

African Cloth

Iron Rods / Bars

Copper & Bronze Manillas

Ivory

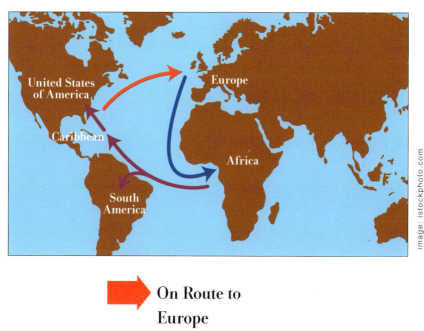

➡️ On Route to Europe

od & Water

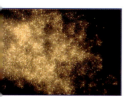

old

Cotton

Cocoa

Caribbean Delicacies

Tobacco

Rum

Sugar

Images (From Left To Right): (1,2,4,7,9,10,11,12,13,15,16) Istockphoto.com, (5,6,8,14,17) Simon O'Connor, (3) Sands Of Time Consultancy

29

Liberated Africans

Africans just after their slave ship was captured.

Who were liberated Africans?

Liberated Africans is the term used here for enslaved Africans formally given their freedom by the British Authorities prior to 1834 or Africans, known as re-captives who were freed by the British Navy from captured slave ships from 1807 onwards. It does not refer to those freed by their slave owners, who were known as free blacks or manumitted blacks.

A child freed from a slave ship.

American War of Independence (1775-1783)

During the war Lord Dunmore, Governor of Virginia, promised freedom to slaves owned by the Patriots (those who rebelled against British rule) and as a result thousands escaped to fight for the British Loyalists forming the Ethiopian Regiment. Despite Dunmore's promises, the majority were not given the freedom they expected. Upon British defeat they were moved to Nova Scotia in Canada and were effectively abandoned. However, British abolitionists wanted to see the promise honoured.

John Clarkson, brother of Thomas, was sent to Nova Scotia to deal with the situation. In 1792 he transported most of the black loyalists known as the Nova Scotians to the new free province of Sierra Leone.

Sierra Leone

In 1787 British abolitionists and philanthropists established a settlement in Freetown (Sierra Leone) for freed slaves. The first settlers were poor blacks mainly from London. They were joined by Africans from Nova Scotia in 1792 and Maroons from Jamaica in 1800. At first, open elections were held to

Wilberforce Memorial Hall in Freetown, Sierra Leone c1900

appoint the officials. Unfortunately this ideal was short lived and in 1808 the Freetown settlement became a crown colony, governed from Britain. In 1821 it was made the seat of government for British territories in West Africa. Unfortunately the Africans were not totally safe and raiding parties did take some back into slavery: Sengbe Pieh (Joseph Cinque), leader of the revolt on the slave ship Amistad in 1839, was captured in Sierra Leone.

Royal Navy Anti-Slavery Squadron

After the abolition of the British African Slave Trade in 1807 and with the formation of an anti-slavery squadron in 1811, the British Navy started to capture slave ships. If these were stopped near to Africa, the enslaved Africans were released at Sierra Leone. Here the Africans known as re-captives could settle back into a life of freedom. The captured ships were sold or destroyed. In total 1600 ships were captured and 150,000 Africans were liberated.

Re-captive Africans in the Caribbean

After 1807 if the Royal Navy captured slaves in the Caribbean they were freed in the Caribbean. As the two main slave routes were to Cuba and Brazil, due to the proximity of the Bahamas and Trinidad the majority of the re-captives were released there. These Africans worked under an apprenticeship, during which they learnt English, Christianity and a trade. These re-captives became productive members of the work force and developed their own communities, reinforcing African traditions.

British Navy crew being killed whilst boarding a slave ship. Many of the British Navy crews were killed or died from disease during patrols.

Slavery in the Caribbean

Brimstone Hill fortress, St Kitts. To protect their trade routes, the European countries built forts throughout the Caribbean. Not only do these forts stand as a testament to the construction skills of the enslaved but also as a statement of control and manipulation of the enslaved populations by the European authorities.

First Slaves

When the Spaniards first started colonising the New World in the 15th Century they enslaved the indigenous Amerindians. Many died from European diseases and there were not enough of the local population to do the work on the plantations. Therefore an alternative work force was sought - Africans.

The slave masters harshly punished the enslaved workers even for minor errors. There was no appeal process and the slaves were at the whim of their owners.

Work

The main plantations in the Caribbean grew sugar, coffee, tobacco, cocoa and cotton. Newly imported Africans underwent a process of adjustment known as 'seasoning' to introduce them to the life and discipline of slavery. At least a third of them died through disease or excessive punishment during this process.

Religion

Christianity, adapted to include African beliefs, was a major part of enslaved workers' lives. This was not without fear for the owners, as it allowed people to gather in large numbers and the Christian beliefs which were preached questioned the doctrines of slavery.

Revolts

There were many slave revolts but the most successful and famous occurred on Hispaniola (Modern Haiti) in 1791. Its leader Toussaint L'Ouverture (c1744-1803) realised that to achieve success he had to ally with Revolutionary France. When Napoleon became Emperor in France, he sought to restore French colonial rule and in 1802 he sent troops to regain control. In 1803 forces led by Jean-Jacques Dessalines' (1758-1806) (the successor to L'Ouverture) were finally victorious over the French and he became the

Sugar plantation, Barbados.

leader of the first independent state led by former slaves.

Other colonial powers also suffered revolts. Jamaica was the most rebellious of the British territories. The runaway slave communities known as Maroons (from the Spanish word, 'cimmarooon' meaning untamed) fought several wars against the British. Nanny of the Maroons was one of their most famous leaders. These Maroon communities also developed in Guyana, Surinam (both of which are in South America), Dominica and Florida where the terrain and vegetation allowed the runaways to hide successfully.

Enslaved labour was replaced by indentured workers who came from India and China. They worked a fixed number of years for the promise of land. Their living conditions were no better than those of the former slaves, and many people lobbied to end this system, including Mahatma Gandhi. It was outlawed in 1917.

Emancipation

On 1st August 1834 slavery was abolished in the British Caribbean and slave owners received £20 million in compensation from the British Government for loss of property - their slaves. The average price of an enslaved worker was valued at about £12. The majority of those freed from slavery had to serve a 6-year apprenticeship, which was intended to prepare them for freedom. In reality it was a transition period to benefit the plantation owners whilst they sought alternative workers. The former slaves gained no financial award or any land to call their own, in fact many of them were worse off. Employers did not always provide housing and punished them unnecessarily, so many left the plantations and squatted on the land.

Eventually campaigning both in the UK and the Caribbean led to legislation which ended the apprenticeship system in 1838.

Former sugar plantation owner's house, Martinique. Today, the plantation site contains a hotel and there are plans to turn the former owner's house into a tourist attraction.

Slavery in South America

Coffee Plantation Brazil, 1850s.

Half of all enslaved Africans were transported to South America.

Brazil

Brazil was a Portuguese colony and over a third of the Africans transported to the New World were settled here. Initially the Africans worked on sugar plantations where life expectancy was only 8 years. However, during the 17th century gold mining became increasingly important. Towns developed and a demand for enslaved urban workers grew as a result of the wealth generated by the gold. After the goldmines became exhausted slave owners started producing coffee.

During the 17th century autonomous African states (quilombos) developed. The largest of these, Palmares was in the deep interior of northeast Brazil and it became a centre of resistance for escaped enslaved workers. It grew to a population of 30, 000 with people working small subsistence farms. Consistently military expeditions failed but eventually the Maroons were defeated and in 1695 Zumbi, the rebel leader of the community, was captured and beheaded. Today Zumbi is still a hero and symbol of rebellion in Brazil where discrimination against black and indigenous people continues.

Many in Britain wanted to see the end of slavery in Brazil not only for moral reasons but because sugar produced here was cheaper than from the British colonies where slavery had been abolished. In 1888 Pedro II, the Emperor of Brazil, eventually abolished slavery, it became the last nation in the Western Hemisphere to do so. Landowners received no compensation and opposition to the monarchy led to its overthrow and the creation of the Brazilian Republic in 1889.

African culture became incorporated into Brazilian life to a much greater extent than in the USA or the Caribbean because in Brazil owners were prohibited from separating slave families. This is reflected in the rhythmic music of Samba, the cuisine of Bahia and the African spiritual religions. But African influence goes far beyond this.

Rebel Maroon in Surinam, 1770s. Escaped slaves formed Maroon communities which played an important role in the histories of Brazil, Guyana and Surinam.

Guyana

In 1763 Cuffy (Kofi), an Akan slave, led a revolt in the Dutch colony of Berbice, in modern day Guyana. Cuffy and over 2,500 slaves held Berbice for ten months, but dissent among the rebels and attacks by the Dutch led to the collapse of the rebellion.

Surinam

Between 1772 and 1777 the Dutch organised expeditions against the enslaved workers who had rebelled in Surinam. Life had become unbearable for the plantation owners in the Dutch territory, as attacks on the plantations were common. The revolt was brutally brought to an end and John Stedman (1744-1797), a soldier who had joined the expedition, recorded the horrors of the treatment of the enslaved. His accounts were used by the anti-slavery movement in Britain.

Punishment of an enslaved female worker, Surinam 1770s.

The River Plate (Modern day Argentina, Uruguay and Paraguay)

In 1786, Spain gave the 'Company of the Philippines' the rights to import slaves into the region of its colonies in the River Plate, Chile and Peru. The company purchased around 6000 slaves a year from British trading companies. However by the end of the 18th century the need for African enslaved labour had declined as the local population was expanding rapidly.

Brazilian Sugar Mill, 1845.

Slavery in the USA

A sanitised view of the cotton plantations in the Southern parts of the United States.

Plantation Life

In the USA, the plantations situated in the Southern States grew cotton, tobacco or rice for profit, and raised crops and livestock to feed the plantation workers. On larger plantations a white overseer supervised the field work and carried out punishments, whilst trusted slaves could become slave drivers, watching over the slaves and enforcing punishments.

THE DIS-UNITED STATES—A BLACK BUSINESS.

The debate over the Civil War in the USA.

Slave Uprisings

There were over 200 slave revolts or conspiracies from the 1600s to 1865. Nat Turner (1800-1831) led the most successful slave revolt in 1831. Turner, an enslaved African preacher in Virginia, and seven followers entered his owner's home and killed the family. They moved from one farm to the next killing all the slave-owning whites they found; other enslaved workers joined them as they progressed. They were intercepted by the militia and white vigilantes who killed hundreds of enslaved workers in revenge. Turner escaped but was captured and hanged two months later.

Enslaved workers were used to keep the cities running. They were used as domestic slaves looking after the wealthy households and as skilled craftsmen such as builders, blacksmiths and carpenters, who were hired out for whatever duties a city needed.

Underground Railroad

Many enslaved workers resisted oppression by deliberately damaging tools, working slowly or by running away. The 'Underground Railroad' was an informal process whereby those who opposed slavery risked arrest or punishment by providing food, shelter and a place to hide, from one 'station' to the next, for enslaved workers who tried to escape. The best known railroad 'conductor' was Harriet Tubman (1820-1913) who had escaped slavery in 1849 and made 19 trips from 1851, helping over 300 people escape to freedom in the North.

Anti-Slavery Movement

In 1775 American Quakers formed the 'Society for the Relief of Free Negroes Unlawfully Held in Bondage'. Although by 1804 the movement was successful in obtaining abolition in the Northern States, slavery

RANAWAY from the subscriber, on the 30th July last, WALTER CALLENDER, an Apprentice to the Britannia and Pewter ware business. He is about 20 years of age, 5 feet 6 or 7 inches high, light complexion, and slender frame. All persons are hereby forbid harboring or trusting said Callender, on penalty of the law: no debts contracted by him, will be paid by the subscriber.   IRA COUCH.
Meriden, Aug. 28, 1835.   4w*88

continued in the Southern States. In 1808 American involvement in the transatlantic slave trade was made illegal and by the 1830s the pressure on the Southern States was extensive. Many freed or escaped enslaved people became involved, including Frederick Douglass, (1818-1895) an ex slave and anti-slavery lecturer and publisher during the Civil war.

Civil War (1861-1865)

The Southern States wanted to separate from the Union of the United States. This led to a civil war fought over a complex of ideological, political, economic and social issues, which focused around slavery. By 1862 the Northern States were losing and Abraham Lincoln, the Northern leader, announced that any runaway slaves joining the army of the North would be freed, and emancipation would be granted to all enslaved workers. On 1st January 1863, the Emancipation Proclamation freed all slaves, even though the war was still ongoing. In 1865 victory for the Union saw the end of the war and the 13th Amendment was added to the Constitution, making slavery illegal.

Black soldiers going off to fight in the Civil War. The Civil War had shown the bravery of enslaved and free blacks as they fought in special black regiments.

Slavery in Britain

West India Docks, London. An engraving by Augustus Pugin and Thomas Rowlandson, about 1810.

Development of the Port Cities

Some of Britain's major ports expanded due to the slave trade. These included London, Liverpool and Bristol. These ports grew to build slave ships, manage the cargoes being taken to Africa to trade for slaves and to house imported cargoes from the Caribbean. As enslaved Africans were taken directly to the Americas from Africa there were no slave auctions in Britain. However there were occasional sales of black servants, almost all children.

Industrial Revolution

The prosperity generated by the crops produced by slaves in the British colonies contributed to the nation's wealth. Those who owned plantations in the Americas formed a strong pro-slavery lobby in Parliament and the law-makers were aware of how much Britain's affluence depended on slavery in the Americas. Profits from the Americas were invested in industry and production of goods to trade with Africa which enabled these industries to develop. How much of this money funded the Industrial Revolution is still disputed.

Somerset Case

Those who brought slaves from the colonies assumed they were also enslaved in Britain. A few black people did go to the courts in London to dispute their status but it remained unresolved until

Statue of Edward Colston, by John Cassidy 1895, located at Colston Avenue, Bristol. Edward Colston (1636-1721) was the son of a prominent Bristol merchant. He was involved in the Transatlantic Slave Trade through trading sugar from St Kitts and as an official of the Royal African Company. Vandals have placed red paint on his name to indicate the 'blood' on his hands.

Detail of one of the plaques on the base of the statue of Edward Colston.

the case of James Somerset. His owner Charles Stewart, a Boston customs official, had brought him to England. He escaped and was then captured and forced on a ship bound for Jamaica. Granville Sharp, (1735-1813) an abolitionist and philanthropist, championed the case of Somerset and in 1772 the case was heard by Lord Justice Mansfield (1705-1793) who agreed that Somerset needed to give his consent before being removed from Britain. This judgement was widely misunderstood. People thought he had freed slaves, but there was no need to do this as they had always been free in England and Wales.

Ignatius Sancho (1729-1780) was born on a slave ship, became a domestic servant and eventually owned his own grocers shop in the City of London.

Black People in Britain

Britain had a large enough work force employed in agricultural labour to make it unnecessary to use slaves for this purpose here. There was a fashion among the rich and aristocratic for black servants as a symbol of prestige and wealth. Others came as mariners, employed either in the Royal Navy or on merchant ships.

There were several famous Africans living in Britain. Ignatius Sancho (1729-1780) was born on a slave ship and became a domestic servant in Britain. He eventually owned his own grocers shop and his letters were published. Olaudah Equiano (1745-1797) bought himself out of slavery and became respected in Britain. He published his autobiography and became the most prominent black figure in the abolition movement. Mary Prince (born c.1788) was brought to England by her master John Wood. She ran away from him in 1828 and was aided by the abolitionist Thomas Pringle (1789-1834) who helped her to write down and publish her memoirs in 1831. There were many others who lived unremarkable lives in a variety of occupations including musicians, gardeners, shop assistants and general labourers.

Olaudah Equiano (1745-1797) bought himself out of slavery, published his autobiography and became the most prominent black figure in the abolition movement.

British Anti-Slavery Movement

The Buxton Memorial commemorates the work of Thomas Foxwell Buxton and the other abolitionists. It was originally constructed in Parliament Square, London, removed in 1940 and moved to its present position in Victoria Tower Gardens, London in 1957.

Campaign to abolish the Slave Trade

In 1787 British Quakers formed the Society for the Abolition of the Slave Trade. The committee included nine Quakers, together with Granville Sharp and Thomas Clarkson who were both Anglicans. William Wilberforce (1759-1834) was their parliamentary spokesperson. Leading African abolitionists in Britain such as Olaudah Equiano and Ottobah Cugoano (1757-?) supported the society.

Portrait of William Wilberforce. He was against women being involved in the struggle. He wrote 'For ladies to meet, to publish, to go from house to house stirring up petitions - these appear to me proceedings unsuited to the female character as delineated in Scripture. I fear its tendency would be to mix them in all the multiform warfare of political life'.

Women, although excluded from the committee, made up 10% of the membership and raised awareness of the violation of family life under slavery.

Clarkson gathered evidence from British ports and his work aided Wilberforce in parliamentary debates and during the House of Commons Select Committee Enquiries. However, the most important

Josiah Wedgwood (1730-1795), potter and abolitionist, produced a ceramic cameo of a kneeling male slave in chains with the slogan 'Am I not a Man and a Brother?' Later, his wife secured production of a similar ceramic brooch, with the caption 'Am I not a Woman and a Sister?'. These two metal anti-slavery tokens show the Wedgwoods' images. Token on the left dated 1795 produced by the English radical Thomas Spence (1750-1814). Token on the right, US Liberty Token dated 1838.

aspect of this campaign was the British population's support. It was the first major civil movement for human rights in the UK. In 1792 the West Indian sugar boycott started. At its height, 300,000 had given up sugar, reducing sales by almost half. Other workers refused to make products to be used in the slave trade.

In 1806 Lord Grenville (1759-1834) formed a new government. He argued that the trade was 'contrary to the principles of Justice, humanity and sound policy' and in 1807 the Abolition Act was passed.

Caribbean and African Influences

The anti-slavery movement was encouraged by events in Africa and the Caribbean. The successful slave revolt in Haiti and failed uprisings in Jamaica showed that an economy supported by enslaved labour was at risk and expensive to protect. Many argued it would be more economic to end slavery and use employed labour.

Sam Sharpe memorial, National Heroes Park, Kingston, Jamaica. Leader of the uprising in 1832.

Campaign to abolish Slavery

Wilberforce believed slavery would gradually end once the African slave trade ended. However as this wasn't happening there were renewed calls to end slavery in British territories. The Anti-Slavery Society was founded in 1823. Members included Clarkson and Wilberforce but women were again excluded from its leadership. In 1825 the Birmingham Ladies Society for the Relief of Negro Slaves (becoming the Female Society for Birmingham) was formed. By 1831 there were seventy-three anti-slavery women's organisations. In 1833 the government passed a bill outlawing slavery in all British territories and it became law on 1st August 1834.

The opposing view

Abolitionists were ridiculed for their "infatuation" that would bring the nation to ruin. There were some high profile pro-slavery individuals including: Members of Parliament; the British Royal Family; and the great military hero of the day, Admiral Lord Nelson, who denounced *"the damnable doctrine of Wilberforce and his hypocritical allies."* and said he would fight to defend *"the just rights"* of the West Indian planters.

Quakers and Abolition

Outside of the Friends Meeting House Winchmore Hill, built in 1790.

Inside of the Friends Meeting House Winchmore Hill, set out for a meeting. (Courtesy of Winchmore Hill Quaker Meeting)

The Religious Society of Friends (known as the Quakers) was one of the major forces behind the abolition of the British slave trade. Their founder, George Fox (1624-91), was so appalled by how slaves were treated in Barbados when he visited in 1671 that he wrote a pamphlet calling on plantation owners to treat them better, although he didn't advocate abolition.

Fox often visited Richard Chare of Winchmore Hill, where he attended meetings and also stayed with Edward and Elizabeth Man at nearby Fords Grove and with Elizabeth Drye, William Shewn and George Watts. Another of the Quakers he visited in Enfield was Thomas Hart who had been a merchant in Barbados.

Burial Register from the Winchmore Hill Meeting House. (Courtesy of Winchmore Hill Quaker Meeting)

Quakerism has been associated with Winchmore Hill since the first Quaker preacher arrived in 1661. Initially meetings were held in Friends homes but later meetings were held in a barn known as Thacker's Yard off Winchmore Hill Green, on land given to the Friends in 1682 by John and Elisabeth Oakley. John was a weaver and silk merchant in the city who had purchased the land for his retirement.

In 1688 a purpose-built Meeting House was constructed and regular meetings were taking place. This house was probably located in the middle of the old burial ground. The present Meeting House was built in 1790, when the previous building had reached the end of its useful life. The money for building the new Meeting House was subscribed by 39 Friends, 22 of whom are buried in the grounds.

It was the only place of worship to be built in the village until the early 19th Century.

Initially there were also meetings held in Enfield which took place in private homes until 1697, after which a house was built in Baker Street at an estimated cost of £60. However as the meeting was never very large it closed in 1794 and the building was sold the following year.

The Burial ground at Winchmore Hill has been in use from the start of the Winchmore Hill meeting. Amongst those buried here who were involved in the abolition of the slave trade are Samuel Hoare Jnr, Joseph Woods, David Barclay and John Fothergill.

Samuel Hoare's grave stone in the Winchmore Hill Burial Ground. (Courtesy of Winchmore Hill Quaker Meeting)

Detail of the Burial Plan from the Winchmore Hill Meeting House. (Courtesy of Winchmore Hill Quaker Meeting)

Famous Quakers at Winchmore Hill

image: Simon O'Connor

Famous Quakers at Winchmore Hill

The local Hoare and Woods families were heavily involved with the movement for the abolition of the slave trade; they were both part of the informal group of Friends who met during 1783 to consider abolition. They were active in the later 1787 London group and organised a dinner party with Thomas Clarkson and Granville Sharp at which they persuaded Wilberforce to speak on abolition in Parliament. As Quakers, their beliefs prevented them from standing as MPs, as they refused to take oaths.

Amongst those buried at Winchmore Hill who were involved in the abolition of the slave trade are:

Samuel Hoare Jnr (1751-1825)

Samuel was on the first informal committee, the Quakers' Abolition Association, which was set up in 1783. Later, in 1787, he became a founder member and treasurer of the London Committee for the Abolition of the Slave Trade. He was also on the Committee set up in 1786 for the Relief of the Black Poor, helping to raise funds to relocate poor black people in a settlement in Sierra Leone. Samuel was a brother-in-law of Thomas Foxwell Buxton, the MP who took over the leadership of the anti-slavery campaign within Parliament when William Wilberforce retired. Samuel remained involved in the campaign to abolish slavery itself after the British slave trade was abolished in 1807.

image: National Portrait Gallery, London

Samuel Hoare Jnr was born at Stoke Newington but is buried at Winchmore Hill.

Joseph Woods (1738-1812)

Joseph was a member of the Quakers' Abolition Association of 1783, one of whose aims was to get articles on anti-slavery published in newspapers and Joseph contributed to these. He also wrote *Thoughts on the Slavery of Negroes*, published anonymously in 1784, which pointed out that all the goods produced by slave labour in the colonies were luxury goods, not necessities.

David Barclay Jnr (1729-1809)

In 1690 John Freame, who lived at Bush Hill in Edmonton, set up a bank with Thomas Gould of Enfield, whose daughter he married. Their daughter Priscilla married David Barclay Snr, a linen draper, and Freame's grandson, David Jnr, became a partner in the family's banking business in 1736. It is often said that David Jnr and his half-brother Alexander were involved in slave trading through Barclays Bank but this is wrong. Alexander was never involved in the banking business. In 1801 David, briefly and for a Quaker, embarrassingly, found himself the owner of a farm and 32 slaves in Jamaica through repayment of a debt. He was quick to grant them their freedom and resettle most of them in Philadelphia with sympathetic employers.

Because of his wealth and influence, David Barclay Jnr was asked for his advice on how to approach the king to gain his support for anti-slave trade measures. In 1773 he led a delegation of Quakers who went to the Board of Trade to try to persuade the Board to consider favourably various anti-slavery petitions from the British colonies.

John Fothergill (1712-1780)

The Fothergill brothers knew Anthony Benezet of Philadelphia, one of the first Quakers to campaign against slavery. In 1763 and 1773 Benezet wrote to John, encouraging him to raise the issue of the slave trade with his patients.

John's reputation as an opponent of slavery became well known outside Quaker circles. He corresponded with Granville Sharp and in 1772, when Sharp was fighting an important case in the courts, he sent James Somerset, the Black man involved, to deliver a pamphlet he had written to John Fothergill. The outcome of the case led to the famous Mansfield Judgement.

John Fothergill (1712-1780) and his elder brother Samuel were Quakers from Yorkshire. Samuel became a preacher and John a doctor with a practice in London.

Parish Churches

St Andrews Parish Church, in the market place, Enfield. A watercolour painted by John Hassell in the late 18th Century, showing the old porch. (EMS Ba1671)

Before 1834, the Vestry (a committee of local parishioners) was responsible not only for the ecclesiastical affairs of the area covered by the parish church but also for such items of lay business as the local administration of the Poor Law and highways.

Each year the Vestry held an annual meeting to elect Churchwardens and Overseers.

Increasingly the Vestry took on the civic responsibilities of local government with the Churchwardens dealing with the upkeep of the church and parish cottages etc and the Overseers who looked after secular welfare. During the 16th, 17th and 18th centuries the present area of the London Borough of Enfield was based on the two ancient parishes of St. Andrews, Enfield and All Saints, Edmonton.

A church existed in Church Street Edmonton by approximately 1136 when Geoffrey de Mandeville gave it to Walden Abbey. But the existing building is essentially 15th century in date built of Kentish ragstone. The south aisle incorporates some Norman fragments discovered during restoration in 1889. Until the early 17th century, All Saints Church, Church Street, was the only place of worship in the Parish of Edmonton. Gradually the population of Southgate increased until in the early 17th century it had reached 200. Previously the inhabitants had to journey to All Saints Church, Edmonton. There

Brass on top of the tomb of Lady Tiptoft in St Andrews Church - dated 1446. Engraving of the brass late 18th century (Ba1616).

image: Enfield Museum Service

All Saints Church Edmonton (EMS Ba1719). Watercolor dated 1845 - thought to have been painted by Dr John Cresswell.

image: Enfield Museum Service

Book of Common Prayer, dated 1635 (EMS Ba469). Donated by the Legett Family. It had been in their possession since 1703.

Weld Chapel, Watercolour dated 1810 (EMS Ba1504).

were no roads, only woodland tracks and paths, which would become impassable in winter.

Up until 1615, when Sir John Weld of Arnos Grove constructed the Weld Chapel, close to Southgate Green, the villagers were compelled by law to attend services at All Saints. The Weld Chapel was a chapel of ease, built to be more accessible to serve the religious needs of the Weld household and the inhabitants of Southgate. It was not replaced until Christ Church was built in 1863 after Southgate became a separate parish in 1859.

St Andrews Church in Enfield Town was the only Anglican Church in the parish of Enfield until 1831. It is predominantly a medieval building. Although a church existed prior to the Norman Conquest, the earliest parts of the building are some 13th Century masonry and a trefoil window in the chancel. The west tower possibly dates from the 12th or 13th century and the nave and chancel arcades date from the 14th century. The 16th century saw both aisles rebuilt and a clerestory added to the nave. The south aisle and porch were rebuilt for a second time in brick in the 1820s.

Bible from the Weld Chapel, 1786 (EMS Ba471). The cover inscription reads: "The gift of Mr James Winbolt to the Chapel of Southgate 1786".

The Parish of Enfield

Market Place in Enfield Town, a hand tinted engraving by Clarkson Stanfield. Dated 1827 (EMS Ba1694).

image: Simon O'Connor

By 1136 a large area of woodland in the North West corner of Enfield had been transformed by the De Mandeville Family into Enfield Chase. It was later under the control of the De Bohun Family who succeeded the De Mandevilles as Lords of the Manor. The Chase was inherited by Henry V whose father Henry IV (formerly the Duke of Lancaster) married Mary De Bohun.

The Chase was to remain Duchy of Lancaster property until the Act of Enclosure of 1777. It was at this time that plots of land were let out on long leases and several large houses were built on the Chase. It was convenient for families who worked in the city to have a country house in Enfield. Until the act, Common rights were enjoyed by the people of Enfield over the Chase to graze cattle, gather firewood and drive pigs to feed on the acorns and beechnuts. These grazing rights were shared by the adjoining parishes of Edmonton, Monken Hadley and South Mimms. In compensation, after enclosure, allotments were granted and used as parish commons for grazing. However the Enfield Parish common

A Cottage at Ponders End dated 1797 (EMS Ba1609). An Engraving by J.T. Smith of a badly decayed house. John Thomas Smith (1766-1833) was a well known engraver and antiquary and later was first curator of Prints and Drawings at the British Museum. As a young man he was employed by Sir James Lake (at The Firs, Firs Lane, Winchmore Hill) as a drawing teacher for his daughter.

Lincoln House, Ponders End (Ba1629). This was a late Medieval/Tudor house which in the late 18th century was a private school. It was destroyed by fire in the mid 19th century.

disappeared as a result of the Enfield Enclosure Act of 1803.

Up to this period, settlement was concentrated around St Andrews Church, the Market Square and Enfield Manor House together with ribbon development of houses along Silver Street and Baker Street as far as the junction with New Lane (Lancaster Rd). There were also houses in Gentleman's Row along Chase Side and Brigadier Hill following the original eastern boundary of the Chase.

Fortescue Lodge (EMS Ba1627). Watercolour, dated about 1810. This was a Tudor property located on Gentleman's Row on the edge of the Chase. It has been demolished and replaced by a pair of Victorian villas.

There was a village at Ponders End with houses along South Street down to the ancient mill (now Wrights Flour Mill) on the River Lee and north along the High Road, with the Durants Manor House set slightly east. Enfield Town and Ponders End were separated by tracts of open land. To the North was Enfield Highway and Enfield Wash with development along the Hertford Road following the Turkey Brook. There were scattered houses to the West around Turkey Street and Bulls Cross.

Beech Hill Park (EMS Ba1521). Sepia drawing dated early 19th century. The land on which this house stands was acquired by Francis Russell after the enclosure of the Chase. Russell was a Duchy of Lancaster surveyor. He named the house Russell Mansion and lived there till his death in 1795. The house survives as Hadley Wood Golf Club.

The Parish of Edmonton

Cottage, Palmers Green (EMS Ba1625). Watercolour, dated 1774. This Farm must have been located away from the main hamlet of Palmers Green, possibly in the Hazelwood Lane area.

image: Enfield Museum Service

In 1801 an act was passed to enclose the common fields of Edmonton. At this time Lower Edmonton was built up around the Green with development along the Hertford Road and south along Fore Street and along Church Street to All Saints Church. Upper Edmonton was a linear settlement along the southern end of Fore Street from the Tottenham boundary as far as Brettenham Road.

Weir Hall, Edmonton (EMS Ba1500). Watercolour dated about 1818. Weir or Wyer Hall is probably of Tudor origin. It was situated on the North side of Silver Street close to Aylward School. In the 16th Century it belonged to the Roman Catholic Leake Family but was acquired by the Huxleys in the early 17th Century. As there were no heirs on the death of the last owner, Sarah Huxley, the house was demolished in 1818.

The eastern edge of the parish adjoining the River Lee was marshy and prone to flooding. In the middle, an area of arable land extended from Fore Street to Firs Lane in the west.

Winchmore Hill and Southgate were heavily wooded and remained so until relatively recently. The largest settlement in the west of the parish was at Winchmore Hill around the Green.

Salisbury House and Bury Lodge (EMS Ba1503). Watercolour. Salisbury House is the only relic of the old hamlet of Bury Street. It was built in the 16th century, a gabled brick and timber house. The interior of a room on the first floor contains wooden panelling and paintings dating to the 17th century. Bury Lodge, the adjoining building, also of Tudor date, which has now been demolished, may have been part of the same property.

Palmers Green was a tiny hamlet at the junction of Green Lanes and Fox Lane with a handful of cottages and a public house. Southgate consisted of a cluster of houses and a public house at the Green with houses extending along the High Street and Chase Side following the western boundary of Enfield Chase.

Minchenden, Southgate (EMS Ba1623). Drawing pencil and wash. Dated late 18th century. Owned by the Duchess of Chandos in 1801. This house was an 18th century property which was acquired by the Walkers in 1853. It was subsequently demolished and incorporated into the Arnos Grove Estate.

On the border of Enfield lay the remote hamlet of Bury Street with clusters of cottages in Marshside, (now Montagu Road) and Tanners End, (Silver Street).

As the City of London was within commuting distance there were a large number of country houses built by merchants which were convenient for the city. These properties can easily be identified on the enclosure map of 1801.

Mr Snells (EMS Ba1518). Sepia drawing. Dated to the early 19th century. This property, situated in Upper Edmonton, has long been demolished but its once owner Nathaniel Snell has given his name to the Snells Park Housing Estate. The estate had been broken up for building by 1849.

Black People in Enfield

> Bap.d August 12. 1788
> ge & Sarah Mayland
> Negro from the Island of Jamaica

The highlighted text is a copy of the baptismal record from St Andrews Church, on the 24th August 1788 of William Johnson. A Negro from the island of Jamaica, aged about 25 years.

These entries from the Parochial Register of St Andrew Enfield are reproduced by permission of the Reverend Michael M. Edge, Vicar of Enfield.

image: City of London, London Metropolitan Archive

Some of the black people in the parish registers may have been servants to the wealthy land owners in the borough, but only two, Taggee London and Mary (a servant to Mr Thomegay), are specifically described as servants. It is rare to find anyone in England or Wales called a slave in official records. Most of the black people in Enfield and Edmonton probably were servants but some might have left their masters to do other jobs.

Some black people were given the same surname as their masters. There were families called Wadeson and Cummings in Barbados in the eighteenth century so Samuel Wadeson and Robert Cummings might have belonged to them but this is not certain.

The Poor Laws

This lack of any special description for the majority of black people in the registers is probably because there was never legal discrimination against black people in England. The colour, ethnic origin or birthplace of some was given in order to make their status under the Poor Laws clear. Parishes had a responsibility to support people who became too poor or too ill to look after themselves. Laws were passed to define who had the right to such support. This was usually through being born in the parish or by working there and being paid for a year.

Clerks carefully recorded any information that might later become important should a person seek financial or other aid. Children inherited their fathers' status under these laws. This is why colour, ethnic origin or birthplace were recorded in baptism and burial registers but almost never in marriage registers: being married in a parish did not give people any rights there. However marriage gave the wife the husband's place of settlement even if she was widowed.

Some settlement examinations carried out in Enfield to determine which parish had responsibility for poor or sick people have survived but there are no black people among them.

Christ Church, Enfield

Christ Church in Chase Side began in 1780 as a small chapel, which was connected with the Countess of Huntingdon's Connexion (a Methodist splinter group). In 1793 Mr Mattias Dupont, the founder of the chapel, took his black servant Mungo with him to conduct a service at Wimbledon. Mr. Dupont died in 1816 but we have no further record of Mungo.

Burials

There are only 11 burials of black people recorded in the parishes for 1536-1840. There may have been other black people here: burial registers for 1789-1806 are missing.

Baptisms in Enfield		
1677	18 May	**Taggee London** a blackamore Lad servant to John Shales Esquire of the parish of Edmonton
1763	17 Oct	**Samuel Wadeson** a negro, native of Barbadoes aged 63 years
1768	15 May	**Robert Cummings** a negro, Native of Barbadoes aged 26 years
1780	30 Aug	**Charles Goa** a Mulatto, Native of Goa aged about 9 years
1784	30 Nov	**John** a negro aged about 20 years
1787	24 Aug	**Mary Helena** a Negro from the Island of St Croix Aged about 27 years
1788	24 Aug	**William Johnson** a negro from the Island of Jamaica Aged about 25 years
1791	4 Mar	**Margaret Morris** a negro Born at Calcutta Aged 14 years
1793	14 April	**John Lees** A negro from St Christophers Aged 21
1793	21 April	**Sarah Lees** a Negro from St Christophers Aged about 18 years
1795	1 Nov	**Edward Williams** A negro aged about 16 years
1796	13 Nov	**Mary Wright** a Negro of Jamaica aged about 50 years

Baptisms in Edmonton		
1686	3 Oct	**Thomas Dungom Indus**
1784	23 Jul	**Elizabeth Peters** An adult negro

Burials in Enfield		
9 Sept 1774		**Mary** a servant of Mr Thomegay
18 Mar 1777		**Hannah Mingo**
23 Aug 1780		**Maria** a negro, Native of Barbadoes aged 26 yrs
20 Dec 1789		**Alexander** a negro (P)
8 Apr 1790		**John Hamlet** a negro (P) a Negro aged about 20 years
25 Sept 1796		**Amelia Johnson** Black woman widow

Burials in Edmonton	
28 Jul 1685	**Samuel Caesar**
20 Jan 1687/8	**Robert Blackamore**
15 Oct 1717	**James Izzard** A Blackamore
20 Mar 1766	**Edmund** A negro

Burials at Southgate Chapel	
30 Aug 1749	**Edmund Blackamore**

The 'P' against the burial entries of two black men stands for "poor". This does not necessarily mean they were destitute. At the time there was a tax on entries in parish registers and the 'P' indicated they did not have to pay the tax because their income fell under a certain level. It suggests they were working and living independently: if they had been servants, their masters would have paid the tax.

Record information courtesy the Church Wardens of All Saints Church, Edmonton

77

Connections with the Slave Trade

Bush Hill Park (EMS Ba1560). Watercolour dated 1834. Bush Hill Park (later called the Clock House). This watercolour shows the house built by the Sambrookes in the 18th century. It was then sold to the Gore family.

image: Simon O'Connor

In the early days of colonisation, three Enfield people are known to have connections with the Americas and with the slave trade:

Humphrey Weld (1546- 1610) of Arnos Grove who bought land in Edmonton in 1584 including a property known as Arnolds Court (Arnos Grove). He took an active part in the formation of the Virginia Company founded to establish plantations in Virginia, North America.

Perient Trott of Enfield (d. 1679), a merchant in the Bahamas. He was a member of the City of London Company of Adventurers to the Somers Islands (the Bahamas were known as the Somer Islands) and also acquired land in Virginia, North America, which was a British colony until 1783. Trott did not work the land but rented it to other people so he profited indirectly from slave labour.

Sir Robert Nightingale (d.1727) of the Rectory in Enfield, spent much of his life in India, returning to the UK in 1708. He invested in a number of merchant voyages and some carried out slave trading. A galley in which he invested was named Nightingale, possibly after him or another member of the Nightingale family who owned plantations in the Caribbean. Sir Robert's banker was James Colebrook, who lived at Arnos Grove, so some of the money invested may have come from him.

Black figure holding a sundial which was moved to Old Park by John Walker Ford when the Bush Hill estate was sold. John Gore had given it to his wife, Hannah (sister to Sir Jeremy Sambrooke) in 1717 on the occasion of their marriage when they were living in Bush Hill Park.

The residence of Sir Robert Nightingale. The Rectory Manor was located on the corner of Parsonage Lane and Baker Street which is now occupied by Monastery Gardens.

The Walker family of Arnos Grove also had indirect links. John Walker married Sarah Chorley whose father was described as 'one of the great West Indian Merchants'. This is likely to mean he was a slave trader, especially as the family lived on the Wirral, next to Liverpool and John Chorley became bankrupt in 1808, the year after the British slave trade was abolished. The Walkers, like the Chorleys, were Quakers. Although from 1761 Quakers were prohibited from profiting from slavery, so much of Britain's business and wealth came from the trade and goods produced by slaves that it must have been virtually impossible for any family involved in business not to have some link.

Murals painted by Gerard Lanscroon in 1723 in the present hallway of Arnos Grove now known as Southgate House.

image: Valerie Munday

Even the poor of Britain indirectly profited from slavery. John Walker was one of a number of philanthropists who used their money, which may have come from the slave trade, to improve the lives of the underprivileged. Among Walker's local schemes was the establishment of the first free school in Southgate and, after the abolition of the slave trade and slavery itself in British colonies, the family contributed generously to local charities.

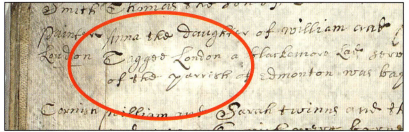

In 1682, John Shales, master of Taggee London (baptised at St Andrews in 1677), sold Bush Hill Park to Sir Jeremy Sambrooke (d.1705), Deputy Chairman of the East India Company (EIC). Jeremy's father, Samuel, had held an important post in the EIC and also had shares in the Royal African Company in its early days, so some of the family's money must have come from slave trading. This entry from the Parochial Register of St Andrew Enfield is reproduced by permission of the Reverend Michael M. Edge, Vicar of Enfield.

image: City of London, London Metropolitan Archive

The Shubrick Family

Richard Shubrick (1741-96), who had a country house at Bulls Cross in Enfield, was the third generation of a seafaring family, all called Richard, who were involved in the slave trade. His grandfather, Richard I, was a sea captain from Stepney in London, who between 1706-14 made four voyages taking slaves from Africa to North America and the Caribbean.

The Quinby plantation house was constructed around the turn of the 19th century on the Eastern branch of the Cooper River in South Carolina. It is thought to have been built by the Shubrick family.

Image: South Carolina Department of Archives and History

Richard I's elder son, Richard II (b. 1707), began his working life as a sea captain and made his first voyage to South Carolina in 1730, probably bringing in slaves. He went into partnership with John Nickelson, who had married his sister Sarah. The Nickelsons owned land along the Edisto River in South Carolina. After her husband's death Sarah returned to England and had offices off Cannon Street in the City of London, where she is described as a "Carolina Merchant" and like everyone else trading with the Americas at this time probably dealt in slaves.

In 1740 Richard II married Elizabeth Ball, the daughter of Elias Ball who owned several plantations worked by slaves near Charleston. One of Elizabeth's sisters Eleanor married, in 1750, Henry Laurens (1724-1792) who was an American merchant and rice planter from South Carolina who became a political leader during the revolutionary war. One of Elisabeth's other sisters married George Austin (born 1710) who was a business partner of Laurens. These interrelated families developed into a distinct community along the eastern bank of the Cooper River which had originally been settled by French Huguenots.

Through her first marriage, Elizabeth Ball had inherited a plantation named Quinby in this area. She died in 1746 and the plantation was inherited by her son Richard III who was born in 1741. Soon after Elizabeth's death her husband Richard II returned to England with their 5 year old son. He married again (Hannah Flowers who was possibly related to Lieutenant General Flowers Mocher, a land owner in Enfield) but seems to have had no children by this marriage. He went into partnership with his younger brother Thomas Shubrick (b. 1710), who

Photograph of the Bulls Cross Manor House, Enfield taken in 1925 just before its demolition. This house was built around 1750 and might have been the property used by the Shubricks as their house in the country.

had settled in Charleston in 1739. The brothers traded in a variety of goods, but also imported slaves from Africa into Carolina. Richard II worked as director for the Royal Assurance Company. When his father died in 1765, Richard III continued the London end of the business with his uncle in Charleston whilst also working in insurance, undoubtedly covering ships involved in the slave trade.

During the American War of Independence (1775-83), when Quinby Plantation was still owned by the absent Richard III, it was the site of a minor battle which was won by British Loyalist troops in 1781. After the war the plantation passed through the hands of a succession of people, including Uncle Thomas, but eventually returned to the ownership of the Ball family.

Richard became the third most important trader with Carolina but the battle to recover debts owed by Americans continued for many years after the war. As late as 1790, Richard was claiming a total of £48,113, worth about £2.3million today.

Thomas and Richard III had offices at 52 Watling Street and later Richard with another partner named Clemson, had offices at 19 Birchin Lane, off Cornhill near the Carolina Coffee House.

Like many rich merchants, Richard III acquired a country house away from City and choose Enfield, where he married Sarah Hotchkis in 1767. They named one of their daughters Carolina, who was baptised in Enfield on 1 February 1773. Her name gives an indication of how important the trade with America was to him. Richard became involved in parish administration in Enfield, serving as overseer of the poor in 1777. He died in 1796 and was buried in Limehouse.

Photograph of the the Pied Bull Public House in Bulls Cross, Enfield taken in 1900. The outside of the building has changed little since it was built in 1716.

83

A Georgian Study

A Georgian Study recreated at Forty Hall in Reception Room 2, during the exhibition in 2007.

image: Simon O'Connor

This room setting represents a Georgian gentleman's study of the period between 1790 and 1820. Its owner is a well-to-do man who has become wealthy as a result of the slave trade. He may be the owner of a plantation in the Americas producing sugar or tobacco and so he may have become rich as a direct result of owning slaves. Or he may be a rich merchant who profited from insurance or has made his money selling goods such as cloth or guns to slave traders in West Africa or by importing the products of slave labour from the Caribbean and North America.

Items from Enfield Museum Service's collection for making and drinking tea. Tea was a fashionable luxury drink and so expensive that it was kept locked in tea caddies. It was served in the finest porcelain tea bowls and saucers. The hot water came from a silver urn and it was drunk with a little milk or cream and sugar.

image: Simon O'Connor

An engraving by Piranesi of the triumphal arch of Septimus Severus in Rome. (EMS Ba1963) Young men of the Georgian period went on extended tours around Europe and were impressed and influenced by the remains of classical Rome and buildings of the Italian Renaissance. This style was often reflected in the architecture and decoration of their homes back in Britain.

image: Enfield Museum Service

He and his family live in one of the larger, grander houses around the small market town of Enfield; houses such as Bowling Green House, Enfield Court and Chase Side House or the smaller Georgian houses of Gentleman's Row. He is well known in town and is influential in organisations such as the Vestry, the Parish Church and the Local Board of Health.

His study is where he attends to his domestic business. The bureau contains all he needs for keeping track of his household accounts, writing personal and business letters and pursuing ideas for new ventures at home and abroad. The card table reflects his interest in cards and gaming and the room is also somewhere he can relax or entertain, drinking wine or rum with his friends and business associates.

There are also signs of other members of the family using the study. His wife seems to have used it as place of respite from the business of running a home to drink tea and indulge in her hobby of painting. The ornaments around the room are signs of the family's wealth and include blue and white Chinese style porcelain, a carved bone box and a pair of crystal glass comports (dessert dishes).

The smooth running of a house like this would have required many servants to do the day-to-day work. It is possible that, with its connections to the slave trade, this family might have had a black servant. They were popular and thought to lend the household an air of glamour and sophistication.

An engraving of Beaver Hall as it was in 1804. The house had been built for the Baring family in the mid 18th century and stood on the south side of Waterfall Road in Southgate, roughly where Chandos Avenue is today. At this time it was the home of John Locke who would no doubt have had a study similar to this one. Beaver Hall was demolished in the 1870s and the land was incorporated into the Arnos Grove estate.

Sylvia Woodcock

Sylvia Sidley, a mixed-race woman, was brought as a servant from India to Cheshunt in Hertfordshire by a Mr Lane. It is not clear whether she was Anglo-Indian or had African ancestry. The Arab slave trade from East Africa to the Indian sub-continent meant she could have been of either ethnic origin and no-one thought it important enough to mention. She had worked for some thirty years for Mr Lane when in 1779 she married a labourer, probably an agricultural worker, named William Woodcock. Seven years later William got a job as a servant in London and Sylvia moved to a house in Enfield Highway, where she did gardening work.

In 1788 William came to see Sylvia and told her he had a job for her cleaning a house in Holborn in London. Instead of leading her to Holborn, William took her via Islington round the outskirts of London to Chelsea which was then a rural village. Here William battered Sylvia savagely and left her in a ditch. He then went back to his lodgings in Westminster and ate supper.

She was found about 3am and a surgeon and an apothecary were called to treat her wounds. She died three days later after a magistrate had taken a statement from her. The parish authorities immediately offered

White Lion Inn, Hertford Road, Enfield Highway. A framed etching dated 1822, by Thomas Rowlandson, (1756-1827) (EMS Ba1692).

image: Simon O'Connor

The journey that Sylvia and her husband might have taken - south from Enfield Wash to Kingsland.

a very generous £20 reward for her husband's capture (most people earned around 15s (75p) per week). Sylvia was buried in Chelsea on 4 November 1788.

A week later William Woodcock was spotted and arrested. Between killing his wife and his arrest, William had married another woman, which must have been his motive for killing Sylvia. He was tried at the Old Bailey in 1789, sentenced to death and hanged. His body was given to a medical school so the students could practice dissection. (At this time it was believed that on the Day of Judgement bodies would rise from their graves, so this was a mark of how terrible his crime was considered.)

This whole episode reflects the general attitude to black people in England at the time in that they were regarded as the same as the rest of the working class. Sylvia's colour is not mentioned in the record of her marriage and not even her next door neighbour and friend in Enfield had thought to ask her about her ancestry. The Parish did not record her colour in the burial register. However the parish authorities in Chelsea went to a lot of trouble and expense both to try to save her life and to track down the man who killed her.

A canteen at Enfield Lock (EMS Ba2024). Early 19th century drawing - Sylvia might have known this canteen.

image: Enfield Museum Service

Durants Manor House, Ponders End, (EMS Ba1626). Watercolour dated 1810. This moated manor house had stood to the east of the Hertford Road since at least the Tudor period and would have been familiar to local people. It had been in the hands of the Wroth Family since the early 15th century. It was destroyed by fire during the 18th century but the Tudor gate house survived until 1910.

Microfiche of the marriage record of William Woodcock to Mary Brock, 6 November 1788 at St Margaret Westminster. The ceremony took place after William had killed Sylvia.

Slavery 1834 to Today

ti-
avery

orrow's freedom

Logo of Anti-Slavery International

Slavery is still a concern today, with an estimated minimum 12.3 million enslaved people in the world in 2005. Different terms are used such as bonded labour, forced labour, child labour and slavery. Today the slave trade is more commonly called 'Human Trafficking', where people are transported under the threat of violence, deception or force. The majority of enslaved people today are found in South Asia, Africa and South America.

Slavery in Modern Britain

No place in the world is free from slavery. Many workers are smuggled into Britain and forced into agricultural work and the sex industry. In 2004 it was brought to the attention of the public when 23 Chinese cockle pickers drowned after being trapped by rising tides in Morecambe Bay. People were not only shocked by their deaths but their lack of freedom and their living conditions. More recently raids on brothels have freed enslaved women from Eastern Europe.

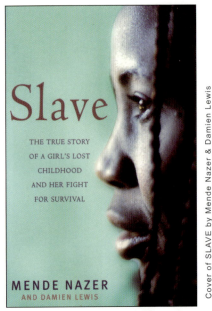

Mende Nazer has published her experiences in the book 'Slave'.

Cover of SLAVE by Mende Nazer & Damien Lewis Reproduced by kind permission of Virago Press

Child Labour

It is the most vulnerable who are prone to being involved in slavery: the poor, women and children. Some families sell children into slavery as they need the money to feed the rest of the family. These enslaved children can work long hours in mines, factories, as domestic 'servants' or in the sex industry. Children are also kidnapped to be used as child soldiers.

World Conflicts - Case Study Sudan

The situation in Darfur, Sudan, highlights that conflicts not only displace millions of people, but open up the local population to all sorts of abuse. The Janjaweed militia (composed mainly of Arab Baggara tribes) has systematically captured civilians from non-Arab farming communities. Women and children have been abducted and sold into slavery in Khartoum and the Middle East. Up to a half million people have been murdered since the start of the conflict but the Sudanese government has covered up the crisis.

What Can We Do?

Many of the goods sold in Europe and North America are produced by workers in the Far East, in conditions amounting to slavery. The legacy of 2007 must be that people are made more aware of modern day slavery and lobby to end this barbaric state. Many people do not see what they can do but even little things will help.

When you buy products do you look to see where they were grown or manufactured? Where possible purchase products that carry the 'fair trade' sticker. Only buy clothing and shoes, particularly trainers, that you are certain have not been made by enslaved workers.

Guilty of Delay Poster. Slavery in the Congo continued till 1909 despite the abolition of slavery in Britain in 1834.

Slavery exists where there is poverty and discrimination and where groups use slavery to maintain fear. We can all lobby our government ministers to encourage greater financial support, aid, expertise, education and opportunities to these areas of the world.

Liberated slaves housed and protected in this free village about 1910. The atrocities in the Belgian Congo raised the attention of the world that slavery was still happening. Campaigns in Europe and the USA forced the situation to change.

Legacy of Slavery

Carnival in Dominica, February 2007.

Racism

For nearly 400 years British people were taught that a person's ancestry was important and that white people were superior. The whole transatlantic slave trade was based on the principal that Africans and their descendents were inferior to white Europeans. It is only recently that the many ways in which black people have traditionally been treated by white people have come to be recognised as racist and a violation of their human rights.

Book page from *The Golliwog's Airship*. The golly image is one of the most commonly known and odious negative images of African descendants.

In 1948 the United Nations, an international organisation that promotes peace and equality, wrote the Universal Declaration of Human Rights, which applies to people in all countries but is not legally enforced. However there are more recent types of legislation that aim to protect human rights. The most widely adopted is the UN convention on the Rights of the Child (1989) and the Human Rights Act (1998). Under the Race Relations Act (RRA) of 1976, the Commission for Racial Equality was set up and the 2000 RRA and subsequent regulations made it unlawful to discriminate against anyone on the grounds of race, colour, nationality or ethnic or national origin.

Sensay at Carnival in Dominica, 2007. This character shows the continuation of traditional celebrations from Africa. The costume would originally have been made from straw.

Women's Suffrage

From 1823 to 1834 one fifth of all the funds for the anti-slavery movement were raised by the numerous women's anti-slavery societies throughout Britain. Despite this women were treated unequally by the male leaders and were even refused a platform to speak at the 1840 International Slavery Conference held in London. Although their priority was still the emancipation of the enslaved, this treatment infuriated many women and it became a turning point for the development of women's suffrage organisations in the UK and USA.

Institutions

The slave trade and associated business activities led to the formation of many companies to sustain the business. This included financial organisations to insure businesses and slave ships, and to underwrite the developing businesses.

Culture

The Transatlantic slave trade was the largest mass movement of people in history and the African Diaspora saw the spreading of African culture throughout the Americas and Europe. As a result, the United Kingdom and Enfield is the culturally rich place it is today. This country is now home to a diverse range of people from different cultural, religious and ethnic backgrounds and black history is very much a part of British history.

Black people have contributed to all walks of life including industry, politics and science. But the most visible manifestation of this legacy is through the influence of African rhythms on many types of popular music from gospel to reggae and hip-hop. This is also illustrated by carnival, masquerade and junkanoo performances that are now common throughout the Caribbean, USA and Europe. These clearly have their roots directly in Africa.

image: Vince Campbell

In 1974, successful local business man Vince Campbell & three others set up Enfield Afro-Caribbean Association to represent the views of black people in the London Borough of Enfield. Later, Campbell together with national and local politicians set up the Community Relations Council, which was to become the Enfield Racial Equality Council.

B'rabbi and B'bookie, Illustration from a story book.

image: Turks & Caicos Islands Tourist Board

Black culture has also been transmitted in less obvious ways such as the popular story telling tradition of Anansi the spider and B'rabbi, a wily rabbit, better known today as Brer Rabbit or Bugs Bunny.

Further Reading and Sources

Slave Accounts

Ferguson, M., (ed.) 1996. *The History of Mary Prince: A West Indian Slave.* Michigan: University of Michigan Press

Gates, H. L., (ed.), 1987. *Classic Slave Narratives.* New York: New American Library-Dutton

Eickelmann C. and Small. D., Pero. *The Life of a Slave in Eighteenth Century Bristol.* Bristol: Redcliffe Press Ltd.

Related to the London Borough of Enfield

Cherry, B., and Pevsner, N., 1999. *The Buildings of England London 4: North.* London: Penguin.

Dalling, G., 1999. *Enfield Past.* London: Historical Publications.

Dalling, G., 1996 *Southgate and Edmonton Past.* London: Historical Publications.

David Olver, A., 2002. *A History of Quakerism at Winchmore Hill.* Winchmore Hill: Preparative Meeting.

Galili, R., 2008. *Arnos Grove and the Walker Family – Isaac Walker The Founder of the Family at Arnos Grove.* Southgate: Southgate and District Civic Trust.

Haigh, D., 1977. *Old Park in the Manor of Enfield.* London: Macdermott & Chant Ltd.

Ford, E., 1873. *A History of Enfield.* Enfield: Enfield Press.

Pam, D., 1990. *A History of Enfield, A Parish near London Volume One – Before 1837.* Enfield: Enfield Preservation Society

Pam, D., 1984. *The Story of Enfield Chase.* Enfield: Enfield Preservation Society.

Stribling J.S., 1917. *History of Christ Church, Enfield.* Enfield:Christ Church

Willcocks, D., 2002. *The Weld Family of Arnold's, Southgate.* St Albans: Dennis Willcocks.

www.oldbaileyonline.org

General on Slavery

Bailey, A. C., 2007 *African Voices of the Atlantic Slave Trade.* Jamaica: Ian Randle Publishers.

Chater, K., 2007 Black People in England 1660-1807 In: S Farrell, M. Unwin and J. Walvin (ed.) *The British Slave Trade: Abolition, Parliament and People.* Edinburgh: Edinburgh University Press, 66-83.

Coules, V., 2007 *The Trade. Bristol and the Transatlantic Slave Trade.* Edinburgh: Birlinn.

Curtin, P. D., 1998 *The Rise and Fall of The Plantation Complex.* Cambridge: Cambridge University Press.

Hague, W., 2007. *William Wilberforce: The Life of the Great Anti-Slave Trade Campaigner.* New York: Harper Press.

Harms, R., 2002. *The Diligent.* New York: Basic Books.

Hochschild, A., 2005. *Bury The Chains. The British Struggle to Abolish Slavery.* London: Macmillan.

Klein, H. S., 1999. *The Atlantic Slave Trade.* Cambridge: Cambridge University Press.

McEvedy, C., 1995. *The Penguin Atlas of African History.* London: Penguin.

Reddie, R. S., 2007. *Abolition! The Struggle to Abolish Slavery in the British Colonies.* Oxford: Lion Hudson,

St Clair, W., 2007. *The Grand Slave Emporium. Cape Coast Castle and the British Slave Trade.* London: Profile Books.

Saunders, G., 1995. *Slavery in the Bahamas, 1648-1838.* Media Publishers.

Shepherd, V. A., 2002 *Working Slavery, Pricing Freedom.* Oxford: James Currey Publishers.

Svalesen, L., 2000. *The Slave Ship Fredensborg.* Bloomington: Indiana University Press

Thomas, H., 1997. *The Story of the Atlantic Slave Trade 1440-1870.* New York : Simon and Schuster.

Thomas, V. M., 1997. *Lest We Forget.* New York: Crown Publishers.

Walvin, J., 1997. *Questioning Slavery.* Jamaica: Ian Randle Publishers.

Walvin, J., 1999. *The Slave Trade.* Stroud: Sutton Publishing Limited.

Walvin, J., 2000. *Britain's Slave Empire.* Stroud: The History Press Ltd.

Ward, W.E.F., 1968 *The Royal Navy and the Slavers. The Suppression of the Atlantic Slave Trade.* New York: Pantheon Books.

Books about Slavery suitable for Young People

Foster, N., 2004. *Out of Slavery.* Bristol: Redcliffe Publishing.

Hatt, C., 2007. *Slavery from Africa to the Americas.* London: Evans Brothers Limited.

Kalman, B., 1997. *Life on a Plantation.* Oxford: Crabtree Publishing.

McKissack, P. C. and F. L., 1999 *Rebels Against Slavery. American Slave Revolts.* New York: Scholastic.

Martin, S.I., 1999. *Britain's Slave Trade.* London: Macmillan Publishers.

Monaghan, T., 2002. *The Slave Trade.* London: Evans Brothers Limited.

Modern Slavery

www.antislavery.org/

www.makepovertyhistory.org

www.amnesty.org.uk

www.eycb.coe.int/compass

www.fairtrade.org.uk

General

Dimbleby, D., 2007. *How We Built Britain.* London: Bloomsbury Publishing Plc.

Index

13th Amendment 45

A

Abolition Act 53
abolitionists 32, 50, 52
Abolition of Slavery 53, 107
Act of Enclosure 1777 68
Africa 12, 14, 15, 18, 19, 28, 29, 33, 48, 53, 86, 88, 94, 99
African beliefs 36
African Cloth 28
African culture 99
African Diaspora 15, 99
African kings 18
African Slave Trade, The 16
aid 76, 95
Akan 14
Alcohol 28
Allada 15
All Saints Church 64, 72
American War of Independence 32, 83
Americas 15, 18, 28, 29, 48, 80, 99
Amistad 33
Anansi the spider 99
Anglo-Indian 88
Anti-Slavery Campaigner 26
Anti-Slavery International 93
Anti-Slavery Movement 50
Anti-Slavery Society 53
anti-slavery women's organisations 53
apprenticeship system 37
Arab slave trade 88
Argentina 41
Arnolds Court 80
Arnos Grove 65, 73, 80, 81, 87
Asante stool 15
Atlantic 18, 23, 26
Austin, George 82
autobiography 49
Aylward School 72
Ayo 15

B

Babylon 18
Baggara 94
Bahamas 33, 80
Bahia 40
Baker Street 57, 69, 80
Ball, Elias 82
Ball, Elizabeth 82
Baptisms 77
Barbados 36, 56
Barclay, David 57, 61
Barclays Bank 61
Baring 87
B'bookie 99
Beaver Hall 87
Beech Hill Park 69
Belgian Congo 95
Benezet, Anthony 61
Benin 14, 15
Berbice 41
Bermuda 27
Bight of Benin 15
Birmingham Ladies Society for the Relief of Negro Slaves 53
blackamore 77
Black history 99
Black People in Britain 49
Black People in Enfield 74
black servants 48, 49
blacksmiths 44
Black soldiers 45
bonded labour 94
Book of Common Prayer 65
Boston 49
Bowling Green House 87
B'rabbi 99
Branding 26
brass 14,15
Brazil 15, 33, 38, 40, 107
Brer Rabbit 99
Brettenham Road 72
Brigadier Hill 69
Brigg Royal Charlotte 26
Brimstone Hill fortress 35
Bristol 48
Britain 28, 33, 46, 48, 49, 52, 61, 81, 86, 94, 95, 98, 107
British 4, 18, 19, 23, 32, 33, 37, 48, 50, 52, 53, 56, 60, 61, 68, 80, 81, 98, 99
British abolitionists 32
British African Slave Trade 33
British Anti-Slavery Movement 50
British colonies 48, 61, 81
British Government 37
British Loyalists 32, 83
British Navy 32, 33
Brock, Mary 91
brothels 94
Bugs Bunny 99
Bulls Cross 69, 82, 83
Bulls Cross Manor House 83
Burial Plan 58
Burial Register 56
Burials at Southgate Chapel 77
Burials in Edmonton 77
Burials in Enfield 77
Bury Lodge 72
Bury Street 72, 73
Bush Hill, Edmonton 61
Bush Hill Park 4, 78, 80, 81
Buxton, Thomas Foxwell 50, 60
Buxton Memorial 50

C

Caesar, Samuel 77
Calcutta 77
Campaign to abolish the Slave Trade 52
Campbell, Vince 99
Canada 32
Cannon Street 82
Cape Coast Castle 23
Capture of Slaves 22
cargo 27
Caribbean 27, 28, 29, 33, 34, 35, 36, 37, 48, 53, 80, 86, 99
Caribbean and African Influences 53
Caribbean Delicacies 29
Carnival 96, 99
Carolina 82, 83
Carolina Coffee House 83
carpenters 44
Casement, Roger 19
Cassidy, John 48
Chandos Avenue 87
Chandos, Duchess of 73
Chare, Richard 56
Charleston 82, 83
Chase Side 69, 73, 76, 87
Chase Side House 87
Chelsea 88, 90
Cheshunt 88
child labour 94
child soldiers 94
Chile 41
China 37
Chinese cockle pickers 94
Chinese style porcelain 87
Chorley, John 81
Chorley, Sarah 81
Christ Church, Enfield 76
Christ Church, Southgate 65
Christian beliefs 36
Christianity 33, 36
Church Street 64, 72

Churchwardens 64
cimmarooon 37
Cinque 33
City of London Company of
    Adventurers to the
    Somers Islands 80
Civil War 44, 45
Clarkson, Thomas 25, 32,
    53, 60
Clemson 83
Clock House 4, 78
cloth 14, 15, 22, 28, 86
Cocoa 29
coffee 36, 40
Coffee Plantation 38
Colebrook, James 80
colour 76, 90, 98
Colston, Edward 48
Colston Avenue, Bristol 48
Commission for Racial
    Equality 98
Community Relations
    Council 99
Company of the Philippines
    41
compensation 37, 68
Congo 17, 19, 95
Connections with the Slave
    Trade 78
conspiracies 44
Constitution 45
conversion to Islam 14, 19
Cooper River 82
Cornhill 83
Cottage, Palmers Green 70
cotton 29, 44
cotton plantations 42
Countess of Huntingdon's
    Connexion 76
Cowrie Shells 28
craftsmen 44
Cresswell, Dr John 64
Crocodile 12
crops 44, 48
crown colony 33
crystal glass comports 87
Cuba 15, 33, 107
Cuffy 41
Cugoano, Ottobah 52
Culture 99
Cummings, Robert 76, 77
curator of Prints and Drawings 68

D

Dahomey 14, 15
Danhomè 15
Darfur 94
Dates of Abolition of Slavery 107
De Bohun, Mary 68

De Bohun Family 68
de Mandeville Family 68
de Mandeville, Geoffrey 64
Denmark 107
Dessalines, Jean-Jacques
    36
Development of the Port
    Cities 48
discriminate 98
discrimination 76, 95
disease 26, 33, 36
domestic servants 94
Dominica 37, 96, 98
Dominican Republic 18
Door of No Return 23
Douglass, Frederick 45
Drake, Sir Francis 18
Drye, Elizabeth 56
Dumont, Pierre Joseph 19
Dunmore, Lord 32
Dupont, Mr 76
Durants Manor House 69,
    91
Dutch 23, 41

E

East Africa 19, 88
Eastern Europe 94
East India Company 81
Edisto River 82
Edmonton 61, 64, 68, 70,
    72, 73, 76, 77, 80
Edmonton Act of Enclosure
    1801 72
Edo People 15
education 95
Egyptians 14, 18
Elmina Castle 23
emancipation 37, 45, 98
Emancipation Proclamation 45
Enclosure Act 68, 69, 72
Enfield 57, 62, 63, 64, 65,
    68, 69, 70, 72, 73,
    74, 76, 77, 79, 80,
    85, 86, 87, 88, 89,
    90, 91, 99
Enfield Afro-Caribbean Association 99
Enfield Chase 68, 73
Enfield Court 87
Enfield Enclosure Act 1803
    69
Enfield Highway 69, 88
Enfield Lock 90
Enfield Manor House 69
Enfield Parish common 68
Enfield Wash 69, 89
England 49, 76, 90
English 33

enslaved 18, 19, 21, 23,
    26, 27, 28, 29, 32,
    33, 35, 36, 37, 44,
    45, 48, 53, 94,
    95, 98
enslaved children 94
Enslavement 20, 22
Equiano, Olaudah 49, 52
Ethiopian Regiment 32
ethnic origin 76, 88, 98, 99
Europe 29, 86, 94, 95, 99
Europeans 18, 19, 22, 98
expertise 95

F

fabric 12
factories 94
fair trade 95
Famous Quakers at Winchmore Hill 59, 60
Female Society for Birmingham 53
Firs Lane 68, 72
First European Exploitation,
    The 18
first free school in Southgate 81
Firs, The 68
First Slaves 36
Florida 37
Flowers, Hannah 82
Fon kingdom of Danhomè
    15
forced labour 22, 94
Ford, John Walker 80
Fords Grove 56
Fore Street 72
Fortescue Lodge 69
forts 18, 23, 35
Fothergill, John 57, 61
Fox, George 56
Fox Lane 73
France 36, 107
Freame, John 61
free Blacks 32
freedom 19, 23, 32, 33, 37,
    44, 61, 94
free men 18
Freetown 32
Freetown settlement 33
French 19, 36
French Huguenots 82
Friends Meeting House
    Winchmore Hill
    55, 56

G

Gambia 12
Gandhi, Mahatma 37
Gentleman's Row 69, 87

103

George I 14
George III 14
Georgian Study 84
Ghana 14, 15, 23
Giza 18
Glass Beads 28
Goa, Charles 77
Goddess of fertility, protector of children and mothers 15
God of Thunder 15
gold 14, 23, 29, 40
Gold Coast 23
Golden Stool 14, 15
Gold guinea 14
gold mining 14
Golliwog 98
Gore, Hannah 80
Gore, John 80
Gore family 78
gospel 99
Gould, Thomas 61
Governor of Virginia 32
Greeks 18
Green Lanes 73
Grenville, Lord 53
Guilty of Delay Poster 95
Guinea 14
Gunpowder 28
Guns 28
Guyana 37, 40, 41

H

Hadley Wood golf club 69
Haiti 15, 18, 36, 53, 107
half guinea 14
Hamlet, John 77
Hammurabi's Law Code 18
Hart, Thomas 56
Hassell, John 62
Hawkins, John 18
Hazelwood Lane 70
Henry IV 68
Henry V 68
Hertford Road 69, 72
Hertfordshire 88
High Street, Southgate 73
hip-hop 99
Hispaniola 18, 36
History of Slavery 18
Hoare, Samuel Jnr 57, 60
Holborn 88
Holland 107
Hotchkis, Sarah 83
Huguenots 82
human rights 19, 53, 98
Human Rights Act 98
Human Trafficking 94
Huxley, Sarah 72

I

Ibeji 15
Ife 14, 15
indentured workers 37
India 37, 80, 88
Indus, Thomas Dungom 77
Industrial Revolution 48
industry 48, 94, 99
Institutions 99
insurance claim 26
International Slavery Conference 98
Iraq 18
Iron Rods / Bars 28
Islam 14, 19
Islamic 14
Islington 88
Italian Renaissance 86
Ivory 28
Izzard, James 77

J

Jamaica 32, 37, 49, 53, 61, 75, 77
Janjaweed militia 94
Jews 18
Johnson, Amelia 77
Johnson, William 75, 77
junkanoo 99

K

Kente cloth 14, 15
killed 19, 27, 33, 44, 90
Kingdom of Benin, The 15
Kingdom of Danhomè (Dahomey), The 15
King Leopold II of Belgium 19
Kingsland 89
Kofi 41
Kumase 14

L

Lake, Sir James 68
Lancaster, Duchy of 68, 69
Lancaster Rd 69
Lane, Mr 88
Laurens, Henry 82
Leake Family 72
Lees, John 77
Lees, Sarah 77
legacy 95, 99
Legacy of Slavery 96
Legett Family 65
Leopold 19
Liberated Africans 30, 32
Limehouse 83
Lincoln, Abraham 45
Lincoln House 68
Liverpool 48, 81

Loading of the Enslaved Africans 23
Local Board of Health 87
Local Trading Vessels 27
Locke, John 87
London 4, 32, 47, 48, 49, 50, 60, 61, 73, 75, 76, 77, 80, 81, 82, 88, 98, 99
London, Taggee 76, 77, 81
London Borough of Enfield 99
London Committee for the Abolition of the Slave Trade 60
long marches 22
L'Ouverture, Toussaint 36, 107
Lower Edmonton 72

M

Mali 14
Mamiwata 15
Mancala 15
Man, Edward and Elizabeth 56
Manillas 28
Manor Houses 69, 83, 91
Mansfield, Lord Justice 49
Mansfield Judgement 61
manumitted Blacks 32
mariners 49
Market Square 69
Maroons 32, 37, 40
Marshside 73
Martinique 37
Mary (a servant to Mr Thomegay) 76, 77
masquerade 99
Medieval 68
Meeting House 55, 56, 57, 58
memoirs 49
Mende 14
Mesopotamia 18
militia 44
Minchenden 73
mines 94
Mingo, Hannah 77
moated manor house 91
Mocher, Lieutenant General Flowers 82
Monastery Gardens 80
Monken Hadley 68
Montagu Road 73
Morecambe Bay 94
Morris, Margaret 77
Moses 18
Mulatto 77
Mungo 76
murder 19, 26

murdered 22, 26, 94
musicians 49
Muslim 14
Muslims 19

N

Nanny of the Maroons 37
Napoleon 36
nationality 98
national origin 98
Nazer, Mende 19, 94
negative images 98
Nelson, Admiral Lord 53
New World 23, 36
Nickelson, John 82
Nigeria 14
Nightingale, Sir Robert 80
Nightingale family 80
Norman Conquest 65
North Africa 19
Northern States 45
Nova Scotia 32

O

Oakely, John and Elisabeth 57
oaths 60
Old Bailey 90
Old Park 80
On Board Revolts 27
open elections 32
Osun 15
Ottomans 18
overseer 44, 64, 83
Oyo 14, 15

P

Palmares 40
Palmers Green 70, 73
Paraguay 41
Parish Churches 62
Parish of Edmonton, The 70
Parish of Enfield, The 66
Parliament 48, 50, 53, 60
Parliament Square 50
Parsonage Lane 80
Patriots 32
Pedro II 40
Perient Trott of Enfield 80
Peru 41
Peters, Elizabeth 77
Philadelphia 61
philanthropist 49
philanthropists 32, 81
Pied Bull Public House 83
Pieh, Sengbe 33
Piranesi 86
Plantation Life 44
plantations 36, 37, 42, 44, 48, 80

politics 99
Ponders End 68, 69, 91
Poor Laws, The 64, 76
ports 48, 52
Portugal 107
Portuguese 18, 23, 40
Prince, Mary 27, 49
Pringle, Thomas 49
pro-slavery lobby 48
profit 19, 27, 44
Promised Land 18
protector of twins 15
Puerto Rico 107
Pugin, Augustus 4, 47
punishment 22, 26, 36, 44
Pyramids at Giza 18

Q

Quakers 45, 52, 54, 56, 59, 60, 61, 81
Quakers' Abolition Association 60
Quakers and Abolition 54
quilombos 40
Quinby 82, 83

R

race 88, 98
Race Relations Act 98
Racism 98
re-captives 32, 33
Rectory Manor 80
reggae 99
Relief of the Black Poor 60
Religion 36
Religious Society of Friends, The 56
Republic of Benin 14, 15
resistance 27
revolt 33, 44, 53
Revolts 27, 36
Revolutionary France 36
rice 44
Rights of the Child 98
River Lee 69, 72
River Plate 41
Romans 18
Rome 86
Rowlandson, Thomas 4, 47, 88
Royal African Company 48, 81
Royal Assurance Company 83
Royal Navy Anti-Slavery Squadron 33
Rum 29
Russell, Francis 69
Russell Mansion 69

S

Sahara 14
St Andrews 62, 64, 65, 69, 75, 81
St Christopher's 77
St Croix 77
St Kitts 35, 48
St Margaret, Westminster 91
Salisbury House 72
salt trade 14
Samba 40
Sambrooke 78, 80, 81
Sambrooke, Sir Jeremy 80, 81
Sancho, Ignatius 49
Sango 15
sanitation 26
science 99
seasoning 36
Sensay 98
Septimus Severus Arch 86
serfs 18
sex industry 94
sexual abuse 22
sexually abused 26
shackled 22
Shales, John 77, 81
Sharpe, Sam 53
Sharp, Granville 26, 49, 52, 60, 61
Shewn, William 56
ship's doctor 23
shop assistants 49
Shubrick 82
Sidley, Sylvia 88
Sierra Leone 14, 18, 32, 33, 60
Silver Street 69, 72
slave auctions 48
slave drivers 44
Slave March 22
Slave post 21
slave revolts 36, 44, 53
Slavery 1834 to Today 92
Slavery in Africa 18
Slavery in Britain 46
Slavery in Modern Britain 94
Slavery in South America 38
Slavery in the Caribbean 34
Slavery in the Congo 95
Slavery in the USA 42
slaves 15, 18, 22, 23, 26, 32, 33, 36, 37, 44, 45, 48, 49, 56, 61, 81, 86, 95
slave shed 17

105

slave ship Brookes 25
Slave Ships 24
slave ship Zong 26
slave traders 18, 22, 81, 86
Slave Uprisings 44
Slave Warehouse 22
Smith, John Thomas 68
Snell, Nathaniel 73
Snells, Mr 73
Snells Park Estate 73
Society for the Abolition of the Slave Trade 52
Society for the Relief of Free Negroes Unlawfully Held in Bondage 45
Somer Islands 80
Somerset, James 49, 61
Somerset Case 48
Songhay 14
South America 29, 37, 38, 40, 94
South Asia 94
South Carolina 82
Southern States 44, 45
Southgate 64, 65, 72, 73, 77, 81, 87
South Mimms 68
South Street 69
Spain 41, 107
Spaniards 36
Spanish settlers 18
Spence, Thomas 52
Stanfield, Clarkson 67
Stedman, John 41
Stepney 82
Stewart, Charles 49
Stoke Newington 60
stool 15
Sudan 19, 94
Sudanese government 94
sugar 29, 36, 40, 41, 53
sugar plantation 36, 37
suicide 27
Surinam 37, 40, 41
symbol of prestige and wealth 49

T

Tanners End 73
tea 86, 87
Thacker's Yard 57
Thomegay, Mr 76, 77
Thoughts on the Slavery of Negroes 60
Tightly Packed 26
Timbuktu 14
Tiptoft, Lady 64
tobacco, 22, 29, 36, 44, 86
Tottenham 72

Transatlantic Passage 28, 29
Triangular Trade,The 28
Trinidad 33
Trott of Enfield, Perient 80
Trunk 22
Tubman, Harriet 44
Tudor 68, 69, 72, 91
Turkey Brook 69
Turkey Street 69
Turner, J.M.W. 26
Turner, Nat 44
Twi-speaking 14

U

UN convention on the Rights of the Child 98
Underground Railroad 44
Union of the United States 45
United Nations 9, 98
United States of America 29
Universal Declaration of Human Rights 98
Uruguay 41
USA 42, 44, 80, 95, 98, 99, 107

V

Vestry 64, 87
Victorian villas 69
Victoria Tower Gardens, London 50
vigilantes 44
Virginia 32, 44, 80
Virginia Company 80
Vodun religion 15

W

Wadeson, Samuel 76, 77
Walden Abbey 64
Walker, John 80, 81
Walker family 81
Walkers 73, 81
Waterfall Road 87
water goddess 15
Watling Street 83
Watts, George 56
wax printed fabric 12
Wedgwood, Josiah 52
Weir Hall, Edmonton 72
Weld, Humphrey 80
Weld, Sir John 65
Weld Chapel 65
West Africa 14, 18, 19, 33, 86
West India Docks, London 4, 47
West Indian Merchants 81

West Indian sugar boycott 53
Westminster 88
What Can We Do? 95
whipping 27
White Lion Inn 88
Who were liberated Africans? 32
Wilberforce Memorial Hall 32
Wilberforce, William 52, 53, 60
Williams, Edward 77
Winbolt, James 65
Winchmore Hill 55, 56, 57, 58, 59, 60, 68, 72
Winchmore Hill Green 57
Wirral 81
women's anti-slavery societies 98
Women's Suffrage 98
women's suffrage organisations 98
Wood, John 49
Woodcock, Sylvia (nee Sidley) 88
Woodcock, William 88, 90, 91
Woods, Joseph 57, 60
Work 36
World Conflicts 94
World Conflicts - Case Study Sudan 94
Wright, Mary 77
Wrights Flour Mill 69

X

Xwéda (Ouidah) 15

Y

Yorkshire 61
Yoruba 14, 15
Yorubaland 14
Yoruba Oyo 14

Z

Zanzibar 19
Zanzibar slave market 19
Zong 26
Zumbi 40

Dates of Abolition of Slavery

Country	Abolition of the Slave Trade	Full Abolition of Slavery
Haiti	Not applicable due to slave revolt.	1791 L'Ouverture lead a successful slave revolt. The state became fully independent in 1804.
Spain	1820	1811, on mainland but continued to use slaves in its colonies.
Britain	1807	1834 the British Empire but the apprenticeship system continued to 1838 and indentured labour through out the 19th Century.
Denmark	1803	1848 (1863 in all its colonies)
France	1818 not effective until 1826.	1848 in all its colonies.
Holland	1818	1863 abolished in Dutch colonies: Surinam and Curacao.
USA	1808	1865 13th amendment outlaws slavery. However all Northern states had abolished slavery by 1804.
Puerto Rico (Spanish colony)	1820	1873
Portugal	1817 not efective until 1836.	1875
Cuba (Spanish colony)	1820 ignored leglislation until 1862.	1886
Brazil	1853	1888

This table is a simplified version of key dates which is only intended to give an indication as despite various treaties some of the countries continued to overtly flout international agreements and through out the period territories changed hands.

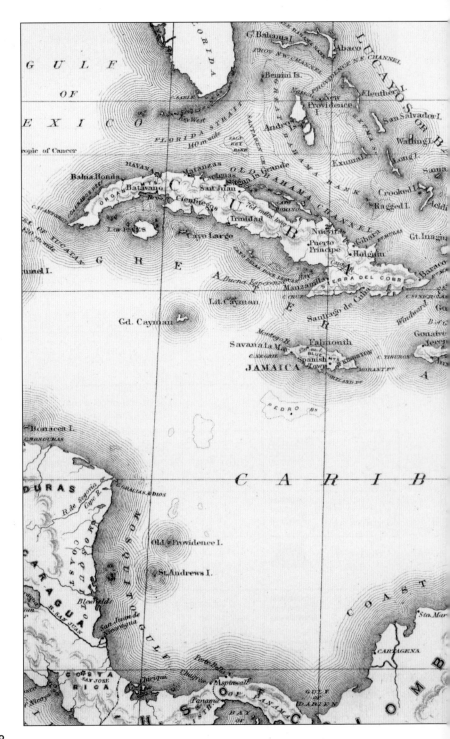